Creative Crafts for Creative Hands

PAPER CRAFTS

CLB 4123
This edition published in 1995 by Tiger Books International PLC, London
© 1995 CLB Publishing, Godalming, Surrey
Printed and bound in Proost, N.V. Belgium
All rights reserved
ISBN 1-85501-597-8

Managing Editor: Jo Finnis
Editors: Sue Wilkinson; Geraldine Christy
Jacket and prelim design: Art of Design
Typesetting: Litho Link Ltd, Welshpool, Powys
Production: Ruth Arthur; Sally Connolly; Neil Randles; Karen Staff; Jonathan Tickner; Matthew Dale
Director of Production: Gerald Hughes

Photographers
Jacket Steve Tanner/Eaglemoss; Jacket flap Steve Tanner/Eaglemoss; Title Page Steve Tanner/Eaglemoss; 9-11 Simon Page-Ritchie/Eaglemoss; 13 Simon Page-Ritchie/Eaglemoss; 15 Steve Tanner/Eaglemoss; 17 Steve Tanner/Eaglemoss 18 John Suett/Eaglemoss; 19-21 Steve Tanner/Eaglemoss; 23 Steve Tanner/Eaglemoss; 25 Ariadne Holland; 27 100 Idees; 29 100 Idees; 30-33 Steve Tanner/Eaglemoss; 34 Marie-Louise Avery/Eaglemoss; 35 Steve Tanner/Eaglemoss; 36 Ariadne Holland; 37 Ariadne Holland; 38 Marie Claire Idees; 39 Mal Stone/Eaglemoss; 41(l) Mal Stone/Eaglemoss; 41(br) Graham Rae/Eaglemoss; 43 Robert Harding Syndication/IPC Magazines; 45-46 Robert Harding Syndication/IPC Magazines; 45-47 Steve Tanner/Eaglemoss; 51-52 Steve Tanner/Eaglemoss; 54 (t) Ariadne Holland; 54 (bl) Steve Tanner/Eaglemoss; 54 (br) Ariadne Holland; 55-58 Steve Tanner/Eaglemoss; 59-60 Simon Page-Ritchie/Eaglemoss

Illustrators
10-12 Christine Hart-Davies; 14 Terry Evans; 16-17 Julie-Ann Burt, Terry Evans; 20-22 Liz Pepperell/Garden Studio; 26-29 Tig Sutton; 30-33 Christine Hart-Davies; 34-35 Liz Pepperell/Garden Studio; 38 Terry Evans; 40-42 Tig Sutton 44 Tig Sutton; 48-50 Tig Sutton; 52-54 Tig Sutton; 56-58 John Hutchinson, Kate Simunek; 60 Kate Simunek

Creative Crafts for Creative Hands

PAPER CRAFTS

*How to make beautiful gifts and objects for the home,
from basic techniques to finishing touches.*

**TIGER BOOKS INTERNATIONAL
LONDON**

Contents

Crêpe paper peonies

Peonies are beautiful reminders of warm summer days. Their extravagant full-blown looks lend themselves well to floral displays, and with their bright colours they make ideal flowers to create from paper. Try making a bouquet to give as a special present.

The peony petals and leaves are simple shapes, so are easy to copy with paper. The lifelike fullness of the petals is achieved by overlapping pre-shaped and colour-tinted crêpe paper sections on to a cane stem. The leaf sections are made from stiff paper and wired and taped to the completed flower stem. Buds add the realistic effect to the display and are easy to make by moulding paper over a cotton ball.

◄ Add a flourish
Brighten up your home by making these wonderful paper peonies. They will add a touch of brightness to an otherwise dull area of a room and are ideal decoration when fresh cut flowers are expensive to buy. You could try making them in other colours.

▼ Looking natural
The petals are gently curved round the central stamens using a pair of scissors.

9

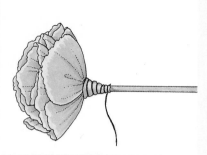

Materials for a peony

Stiff smooth paper in leaf green 4 x 64cm (1½ x 25¼in).
Crêpe paper in crimson 50 x 70cm (19¾ x 27½in), yellow 25 x 5cm (10 x 2in) and leaf green 8 x 6cm (3¼ x 2¼in).
Pastel crayon in pale pink.
Split bamboo cane 45cm (17¾in) long.
Florist's stem wire 15cm (6in) long.
Soft floral wire and **green floral tape**.
Clear adhesive such as Uhu glue.

MAKING A PEONY

1 Cutting the leaves Fold smooth paper strip in half lengthways and using the template, cut 5 leaves.

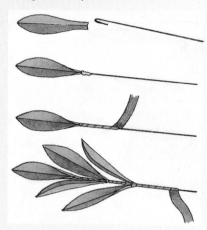

2 Making a stem of leaves Bend down 1cm (⅜in) at one end of the stem wire, glue the end of a leaf to the bent end of the wire. Bind with tape to cover join, then stretching the tape slightly, continue taping the stem taking in pairs of leaves.

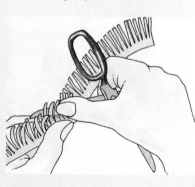

3 Making the stamens Using scissors fringe the strip of yellow crêpe paper to 12mm (½in) from the edge, then curl the fringes by stretching them between thumb and scissor blade.

4 Attaching the stamens Spread the glue over about 12mm (½in) at the end of the cane. Wind the un-cut edge of the fringe around the glued end of cane, then bind with the soft wire to secure.

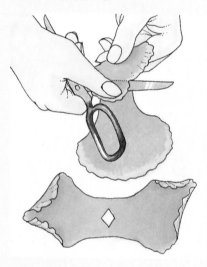

5 Cutting the peony petals Using the template and noting the grain of the paper, cut twelve pieces. Gently crayon the petal edges along both sides of the top curves. Curl the petals as for the stamens.

6 Making the peony Thread one petal shape up the cane, gather round the stamen and bind with the soft wire. Repeat with remaining petals, positioning each petal over the space between previous petals.

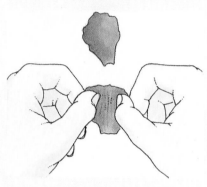

7 Cutting the calyx pieces Using the template and noting the grain of the paper, cut two calyxes from the green crêpe paper. Cup the calyxes by stretching with your thumbs.

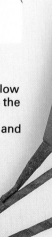

8 **Attaching the calyxes** Dab a little glue to the end of each calyx and position each side of the flower base.

9 **Binding the stem** Beginning at the calyx, slightly stretching the tape, bind the tape around the stem taking in the stem of leaves as you work.

tip

Clever arrangements
Once made you could use the paper peonies as a special flower arrangement in a bowl or a favourite vase.

Materials for the peony bud
Smooth stiff paper in leaf green 4 x 12cm (1½ x 4¾in).
Crêpe paper in crimson 10 x 10cm (4 x 4in) and leaf green 8 x 6cm (3¼ x 2¼in).
Paper bead 25mm (1in) in diameter.
Split bamboo cane 45cm (17¾in) long.
Soft floral wire and **green floral tape**.
Clear adhesive such as Uhu glue.

MAKING A PEONY BUD

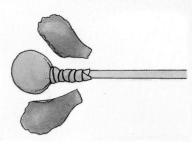

1 **Making the bud** With the glue stick the paper bead on to the end of the cane. Using the template and noting the grain of the paper, cut a piece of crimson crêpe paper for the bud. Stretching the crêpe paper to fit, cover the bead and then bind paper round stem with the soft wire to secure.

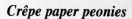

2 **Attaching the calyxes** Using the template and noting the grain of the paper, cut two pieces of green crêpe paper and attach to base of bud as for peony flower.

3 **Binding the stem** Beginning at the calyx, slightly stretching the tape, bind the tape around the hem taking in the leaf as you work.

CRÊPE PAPER PEONIES
Pattern pieces – actual size

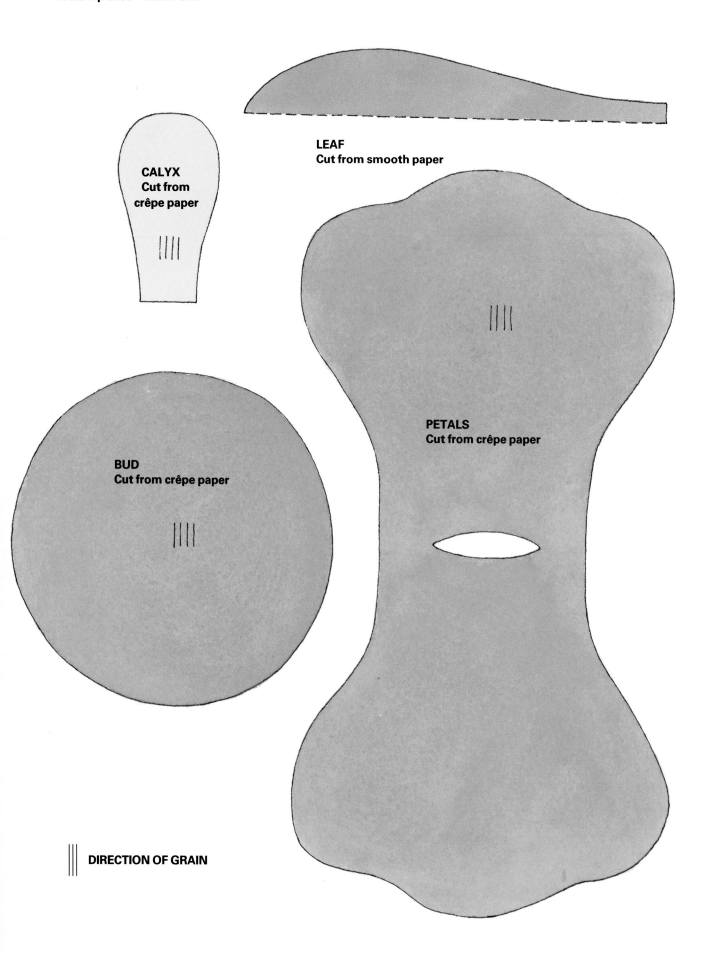

CALYX
Cut from crêpe paper

LEAF
Cut from smooth paper

BUD
Cut from crêpe paper

PETALS
Cut from crêpe paper

||| **DIRECTION OF GRAIN**

Cut paper tablecloth

A paper tablecloth, with straight edges, often looks dull. A cut-out border around the edge will instantly make it look more attractive. If the tablecloth is then laid over a slightly larger one in a contrasting colour, the cut-out motifs will be highlighted. Choose as heavy a weight of paper cloth as possible – very light, flimsy paper tends to tear easily.

Once you have mastered the cut-out technique, working through several layers of paper, you can experiment with designs to suit various occasions.

Materials
Paper tablecloth any size.
Tracing paper and **white paper** to make the pattern.
A pencil and long **ruler**.

Craft knife and **sharp scissors**.
Masking tape and **dressmakers' pins** to hold layers together.
Iron and **tissue paper** to press cloth.

▼ Threaded ribbon and bows
The bow motif is centred on the sides and then set at a jaunty angle across the corners. The threaded ribbon effect is then cut between.

MAKING THE CUT OUT BORDERS

1 Enlarging the motif Draw a grid of 2cm (¾in) squares on white paper and enlarge the motif given on the right. Add the bold guidelines at right-angles at the corners, to help positioning.

2 Tracing the motif Fold the tablecloth in half and then into quarters. Match the bold guidelines on the pattern to the edges of the paper cloth and, using tracing paper, carefully transfer the enlarged motif on to the corner of the cloth. Remove the white paper pattern and tracing paper and place a cross on each section of the motif to be cut out.

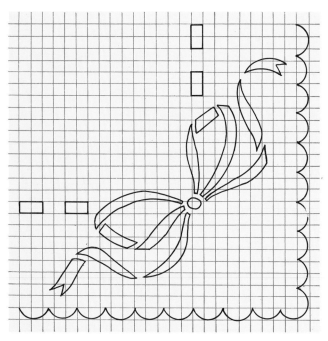

3 Cutting out the corner motif Place the corner of the folded tablecloth on to a cutting board and secure with masking tape. Using a craft knife, and working through all four layers at once, cut out the areas of the bow and threaded ribbon marked with an 'X' in the diagram to Step 1.

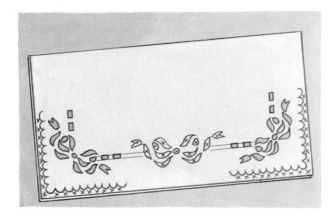

4 Cutting out the centre bow motifs Open out the tablecloth so that it is folded in half and draw two parallel lines between the threaded ribbon cut-outs. Mark the centre point and place the pattern with the knot of the bow at this point. Transfer the bow motif, remove the pattern and, working through both layers, use the craft knife to cut out the motif.

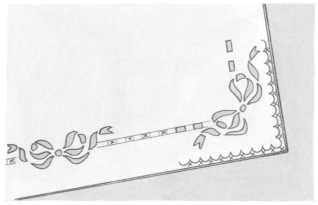

5 Cutting out the threaded ribbon Mark off the ribbon sections at right-angles between the two parallel lines at about 2cm (¾in) intervals. Then mark every other section with a cross. Using the craft knife cut out the marked areas.

6 Completing the border Unfold the cloth and re-fold in half at right-angles to the first fold. Placing the bow motif in the centre and marking the threaded ribbon as before, cut out the marked areas through both layers of the paper.

7 Marking the edge Fold the tablecloth into quarters along the original folds. Using the scallops already transferred as a guide, continue the scalloped edge to the fold checking that a whole scallop ends at the fold or that the fold cuts the scallop exactly in half. This ensures that the scallops are not distorted.

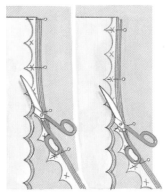

8 Cutting the edge Pin the four layers of paper together between every couple of scallops and, holding the paper in your free hand, use scissors to carefully cut out the scalloped edge. Open out the cloth to press. Place tissue paper over the tablecloth and use a warm, dry iron to smooth out the creases.

Pricked paper lampshades

F lat paper lampshades have a simple shape and delicate appearance of irresistible charm. Their infinite variety and the possibilities they offer for decorative treatments make them all the more appealing – they can be hand-painted, marbled, stencilled, or pricked into pretty lacy designs, for example. As a final touch, they can be finished with lace, braid or bias binding.

The method for making flat paper lampshades is the same, no matter what decorative technique you use. The paper or card is cut to shape from a pattern, decorated and then glued to the frame. This frame can be any size, but it must have straight struts and circular rings. Drum-shaped shades are the easiest to cover, but tapered drums (empire) or even coolie shades can be used.

Choosing the card

Any firm card or paper is suitable for a paper shade, provided that it is quite strong and has a certain amount of flexibility. Good quality, 300 gramme (10½oz) watercolour paper has the required qualities and is readily available. It has an off-white colour which produces an attractive, warm light when the lamp is lit. Parchment, although more difficult to find, is an interesting alternative. It has a mottled, slightly opaque appearance, which is very pretty and quaint.

Choosing the trimmings

Trimmings are the final touch on paper lampshades, whether you have made them yourself or bought them ready-made. On homemade lampshades they have the added advantage of covering the rough edges and any marks where the glue has gone over the edge.

A plain bias binding, matching the colour of the paper or card, is the subtlest trimming, and because the binding stretches, it is also the easiest to smooth in place on a steeply sloping shade. Where the paper or card has been stencilled or painted, a coloured binding or a trimming of ribbon or braid can be used to highlight a particular colour.

▼ *Pricked paper shades*
Economical and fun to make, these paper lampshades are trimmed with fine lace and decorative cord. The pricked bow motif was inspired by the pattern of the lace trimming.

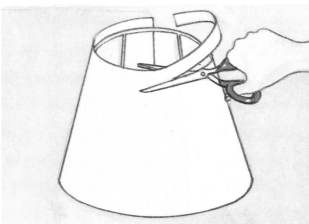

Materials
Drum, empire or coolie frame.
Thick paper or card.
Sheet of brown paper to make a pattern.
Scissors or craft knife and **paper glue.**
Trimmings.
Clothes-pegs or bulldog clips.

MAKING A FLAT PAPER SHADE

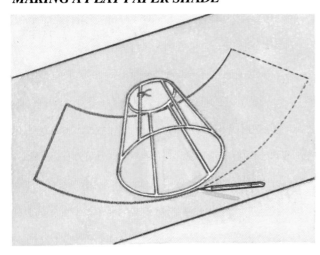

1 Make a paper pattern Place the frame on a large sheet of brown paper – you can tape several sheets together if necessary. Draw a line on the paper along one of the struts, then roll the frame across the paper, drawing along the bottom ring as you go. Stop when you get back to the original strut. It may help to mark the strut by knotting a strand of coloured thread round it.
 Return to the beginning, line up the strut, and roll the frame again, this time drawing along the top ring. Make sure the bottom ring is following the line you have already drawn. Draw along the strut at the other end, then cut out the pattern adding 1cm (⅜in) all round.

2 Trim to fit Using clothes-pegs or bulldog clips to hold the brown paper pattern to the frame, trim the pattern at top and bottom to fit exactly. The pattern should overlap on itself by 2cm (¾in) for the join. Trim the overlap as necessary to make sure it is an even width all the way down – when the light is lit, an uneven overlap will show.

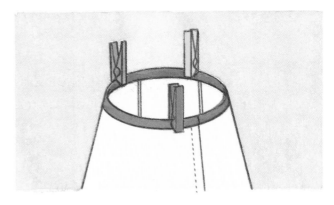

3 Cut out and fit Cut out the paper or card using your brown paper pattern as a guide, adding about 1cm (⅜in) to top and bottom. Decorate the card if you wish. Fold the card round the frame and mark the overlap lightly in pencil. Apply the glue sparingly and stick together at the overlap. When dry, place the shade on the frame and trim off any excess card as necessary.

4 Binding trim If you wish, fold ready-made bias binding or ribbon in half lengthways and then glue to the top and bottom edges. Turn the second end of the binding or ribbon under so that it overlaps the first end slightly; glue. Clothes pegs can be used to secure the binding while the glue dries.

5 Attaching the shade Glue the shade to the frame using rubber solution glue, and making sure the overlapped join runs along one of the struts. If not using binding to neaten the raw edges, glue on a ribbon or braid trim. Use a low wattage bulb on the lamp to prevent the paper from singeing.

A PRICKED PATTERN

A pricked pattern is a very pretty but unusual decoration for a flat paper lampshade. The design can be just one motif, centred on the front of the shade, or a simple pattern, which encircles the shade. It can even be done as a border.

1 Planning the design Choose your design carefully, using magazine pictures or fabrics for inspiration, or copy the bow template we used. Experiment on the lampshade pattern to find the most attractive arrangement and size of needle to produce the effect you prefer.

▲ **Delicate bow**
A medium-sized needle produces a delicate pricked pattern. Use a darning needle for bolder results.

▼ **Bow template**
Here is the template used on the shade above. Enlarge it on a grid or photocopier to the size you require.

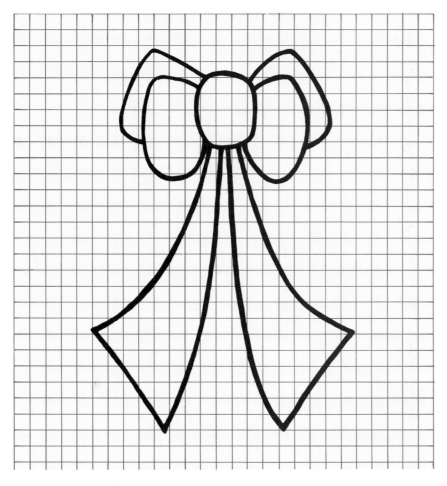

2 Pricking the design Cut out the shade from plain card or thick paper, and place it right side up on a blanket-covered table. Position the design on top and hold in place with masking tape. Prick out the pattern using a reasonably thick needle. Try to space the holes evenly and make them the same size.

3 Attaching the shade Glue the shade as in step 3 for a flat paper shade; leave to dry and attach to the frame as before. Trim to fit and add decorative trimmings.

Accurate positioning
To help to ensure that the pricked pattern is positioned accurately, lightly mark the card at the top and bottom of each strut when you first fit it. Use these marks as a reference to help to keep the design central, otherwise the design may be positioned at an angle in the finished shade.

Pricked and cut patterns

On drum-shaped lampshades, finding a pattern for the pricked design is easy. You can take a motif from fabric used elsewhere in the room, or use a pattern from a book for inspiration. Choose a single motif, to be repeated round the shade, or opt for a continuous design or even a scene, such as the delightful farmyard setting on the shade shown right.

The shape of a coolie or empire shade makes it more difficult to design a pattern that looks right. Single, repeated motifs are easiest to do, and fill the area best if they are wider at the bottom than at the top. If you prefer, use several simple motifs to fill the space attractively, or take the plunge and do a freehand design, using the brown paper pattern to plan the design and experiment on.

▼ Expert ease
Even on empire shades, the experts make continuous patterns look easy. This bold pattern has a mirror image reflected on each side of the shade.

▶ Pierced variation
Advanced patterns, based on the pricked paper shade, can be made using a craft knife and punch. A lining of grease-proof paper gives this shade a warm glow.

18

Paper medallions

These paper medallions use a combination of good quality art paper and an attractive cut out design to achieve a stunning effect. They look superb if hung in a window where the light can shine through the design, especially as the curling of the cut sections gives a three dimensional effect, softening the sharp edges with the shadows. The cut out design is backed with tracing paper which has the effect of softening the shadows.

The medallions are set in small round handbag rings which are available from craft shops or large department stores. They have been given an attractive two-colour sponged paint finish and hung with a fine satin ribbon. Choose a colour scheme to match the decoration in the room you intend to hang them in.

Once you have mastered the technique of cutting paper outlines using the trace patterns given on page 22, you will find it easy to adapt designs found in magazines or even to create your own simple cut-out patterns.

▼ Hanging in the light
A few curved cuts and pinpricks suggest the delicate hanging flowers of the fuchsia in the medallion on the left. The lovebirds on the right are taken from the traditional willow pattern china design. Look for designs which use soft curved lines rather than sharp angles as they are easier to cut.

Fuchsia and willow pattern medallions

The technique for making the fuchsia flowers and bud picture is the same as for the willow pattern design. The medallion has a mint green frame with a matching ribbon loop and bow. Hung in a window to catch the light, the effect is springlike.

Materials

A heavy textured **watercolour paper** such as Bockingford, 20cm (8in) square

Tracing paper 2 sheets 20cm (8in) square.

Plastic handbag ring 12.5cm (5in) in diameter.

Small eyelet screw

Narrow satin ribbon 3mm (⅛in) wide and 40cm (16in) long

Emulsion 1 tester pot for basecoat

Artist's acrylic paint 1 tube to contrast with emulsion

Small natural sponge

Craft knife and **sharp paper scissors**

Masking tape and **bradawl**

Pin, large needle and **UHU glue** and **Pritt glue stick**

Fine glasspaper grade 000

Large knitting needle

Thick cardboard to use as a cutting mat

HOW TO MAKE THE MEDALLIONS

1 Painting the frame basecoat Rub the handbag ring with the glasspaper to roughen the surface. Coat the ring with 3 layers of emulsion, allowing the paint to dry thoroughly between each coat.

2 Sponging the frame Mix a little acrylic paint with a small amount of emulsion in a saucer and then dilute with a few drops of water to the consistency of the emulsion. Dip the sponge into the paint mixture, squeeze to remove most of the paint, then dab over the ring and allow to dry.

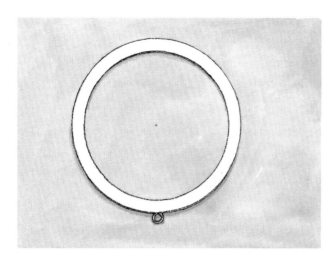

3 Attaching the eyelet screw Using the bradawl make a small hole on the outside edge of the ring. Screw the eyelet into this hole.

4 Transferring the design Using the tracing paper, transfer the fuchsia design on to the wrong side of the watercolour paper.

5 Cutting out the design Place the water colour paper right side down on the cutting surface and hold in position with masking tape. Using the tip of a craft knife, cut along all the lines and cut out the marked sections except the dots.

6 Pierce the holes From the wrong side use a pin to pierce a hole at each dot. Turn the design over and, from the right side of the work, enlarge the holes marked with a larger dot with a large knitting needle.

7 **Curving the design shapes** From the right side of the work, using the knitting needle, carefully push each cut area to the wrong side and then gently curve the flaps away from the work with your fingers. This will soften the outlines of the cut edges.

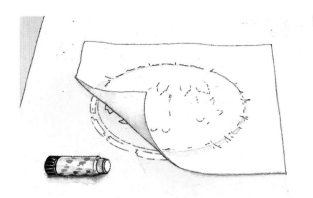

9 **Cut out the medallion** Using the scissors, carefully cut out the medallion around the outline through both layers of paper.

10 **Frame the medallion** Working from the right side and using a strong glue such as UHU, draw a line of adhesive close to the edge around the medallion. With the eyelet screw at the top of the design, carefully glue the sponged ring to the medallion.

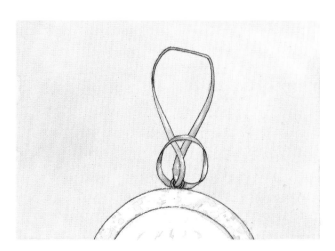

8 **Attaching the backing** Using a paper glue such as Pritt glue stick, draw a line of glue on the wrong side just within the circular outline. Lay a piece of tracing paper over the design and, taking care not to flatten the cut outs in the pattern and gathering as necessary around the outline, stick the tracing paper to the cut out design.

11 **Making the hanging loop** Cut a 30cm (12in) length of ribbon and glue the two ends together. Allow to dry and then with the join at one end, fold the ribbon in half and pass the unjoined end through the eyelet screw from the back of the work and then through the joined end and draw up, so that the ribbon loops over itself.

12 **Making the bow** With the remaining 10cm (4in) of ribbon, make a bow and glue into place over the joined ends of the hanging loop.

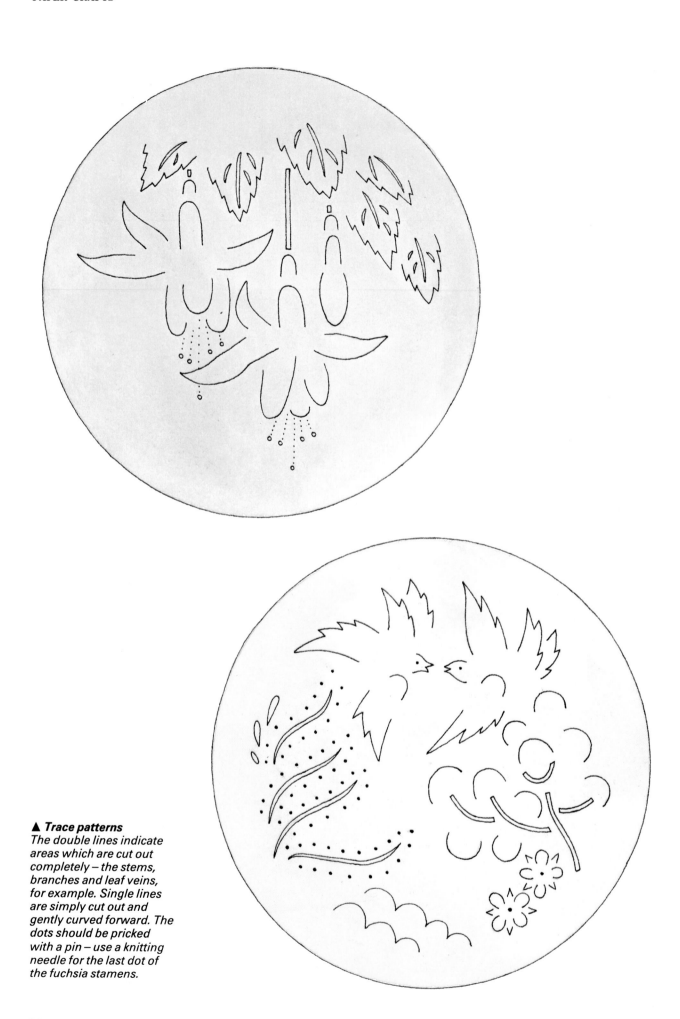

▲ Trace patterns
The double lines indicate
areas which are cut out
completely – the stems,
branches and leaf veins,
for example. Single lines
are simply cut out and
gently curved forward. The
dots should be pricked
with a pin – use a knitting
needle for the last dot of
the fuchsia stamens.

Papier mâché bowls

Papier mâché is a simple craft that can be used to make beautiful objects from readily available materials that cost next to nothing. The painted motifs give the bowls a stunning, original look, and they are so easily added. Simply paint or stencil your design on to flat sheets of paper, select the best, cut them out and then stick them on to the bowl using the same papier mâché technique as before. You can make the design as busy or simple as you like.

Materials

Mould use a china bowl or plate
Clear film wrap
Vaseline
Kitchen towel
Newspapers
Wallpaper paste
Fine white typing paper
Heat-proof bowl
Tea bags x 3
Iron and **ironing board**
Paintbrush 2.5cm (1in) wide
Fine paintbrush
Sharp scissors
Ruler and **HB pencil**
Oil based model paint black and other assorted colours
Clear spray varnish

MAKING THE BOWL

1 Prepare the finishing paper Place the tea bags into the heat proof bowl, pour boiling water over them and leave to stand for 5 minutes. Scrunch up some of the white typing paper and immerse in the tea leaving completely covered for a minute. Remove the paper, smooth out and leave to dry. Cover the ironing board and iron the paper flat. It should now have a faded crinkly look.

2 Preparing the mould Apply a layer of Vaseline over the side of the mould to be used, then cover with clear film wrap, overlapping the edges of the mould. Fold a piece of kitchen towel into a small pad and use it to smooth out any wrinkles or bubbles in the cling wrap.

3 Prepare papier mâché materials Tearing the newspaper against the edge of the ruler, rip it into strips 2.5cm (1in) wide and 10cm (4in) long. Follow the packet instructions for wallpaper paste, mix as for lining paper and leave to stand for a while.

4 Papier mâché the mould Using the wider brush, freely paste a strip of newspaper and apply to centre of mould. Overlapping each strip, work outwards and, keeping the rim shape, cover the mould with one layer. Apply two more layers in different directions. Now apply layers of plain white paper until no newsprint shows; press out any air bubbles. Leave the bowl to dry.

5 Remove from the mould Use the edges of the film wrap to ease the papier mâché bowl away from the mould; remove the film wrap. Layer the outside with white paper strips, finishing with a coat of glue inside and out. If necessary, carefully trim the bowl rim with sharp scissors.

6 Painting the motifs You can use our motifs for inspiration, or if you prefer why not design your own. You will find animal shapes are fairly easy to draw. Paint several motifs on to sheets of tea-dyed paper using the fine paintbrush and model paint. Leave the sheets of tea-dyed paper until they have dried completely.

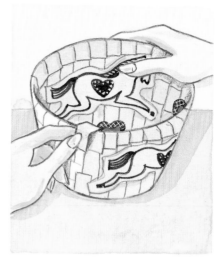

7 Decorating the bowl Tear round the motifs carefully to separate them; scissor cut edges would be too sharp. Rip the remaining tea-dyed finishing paper into strips. Space the best motifs evenly over the inside and outside of the bowl, and paste them in position. Then fill in the spaces with tea-dyed paper; paste the strips over the rim and around motifs. Set aside until dry.

8 Finishing the bowl Decorate the rim with tiny spots of paint and leave to dry. Then spray a coat of varnish over the bowl. Once the first coat is dry, apply a second coat and leave the bowl to dry.

Making it easy
To keep a check on whether you have applied a complete layer of paper, why not use a different coloured paper for each layer, such as the pink coloured Financial Times, and the Yellow Pages.

Découpage decoration

Découpage is a traditional craft in which paper motifs are stuck to objects and then layers of varnish are applied to produce a lacquer-like finish. By carefully arranging motifs, a simple box can be made into something special.

Choosing your papers
Pick your papers carefully. They must be of a reasonable thickness to withstand layers of varnish and they should be printed on one side only – otherwise the underside will show through to the surface after gluing. For this reason it's best to avoid thin papers such as magazine pages – the varnish tends to make the printing show through the paler colours; choose the more substantial wrapping papers and greetings cards or ready-made cut-outs.

▼ Victorian motifs
Craft shops sell special découpage paper and Victorian-style decals – the paper shapes designed for scrap books shown here. Victorians would use programmes and postcards or collect motifs on a theme, such as birds or flowers, and spend evenings covering objects ranging from folding screens to photograph albums.

Découpage and accessories

Lamp bases, small coffee tables, fire screens and any type of box can be transformed with découpage. This treatment works well when a group of objects – designed to be seen together – are decorated to follow a particular theme or to complement a colour scheme in the room.

Covering a table Prepare and paint a small table in a colour to blend subtly with the découpage motifs. Water-based paints can be used for speed, as protective coats of varnish provide a durable finish. Cut out a selection of paper shapes, and try out different effects. Work corner motifs over or under adjacent shapes.

Decorating containers
Flower pots and vases are good subjects for découpage, provided the motifs are small enough to stick to curves without creasing – each shape should stick flat against the background.

For an all-over design, cut out a choice of motifs and arrange them in a line around the container to enhance the shape. Add motifs until the surface is covered.

Decorating a screen Make a simple panelled screen into an important decorative feature using a selection of découpage motifs. The design will have extra impact if the motifs are specifically selected from a limited colour palette, and are arranged so that they fill each section of the panel in an informal, 'growing' way.

Make the design on each panel slightly different, to accentuate the lively effect of the flourishing découpage. The design could flow from one panel to the next, or into the centre from the sides, for example, or perhaps it could grow up from the base of the screen, with foliage and stems expanding into radiant blooms at the top.

Adding motifs to boxes
Make cardboard boxes into presentable containers with découpage. For the best results, plan motifs so they trail over the edges to the lid sides – paste motif overlaps to the inside of the lid and decorate the box lining too. Match up the motifs on the sides of the lid with those on the box sides for a visual balance.

Découpage designs with wallpaper

Découpage has traditionally been reserved as a decoration for furniture and small objects like trinket boxes and trays. Originally inspired by the elaborately detailed and expensive, lacquered furniture imported during the seventeenth and eighteenth centuries from China and Japan, the craft developed as a way of imitating the designs with less costly paper and varnish. The Victorians were particularly fascinated with découpage, which became a favourite pastime. They decorated everything with precut paper shapes, featuring popular themes like flowers.

Découpage need not be limited to traditional applications, and today it is coming into its own in contemporary interior decoration. You will find many wallpaper designs offer inspiration for decoration on a larger scale and with a variety of subject matter. Mural effects,

▲ Ring-o'-roses
This pretty 'porthole' window has been embellished with a frame of blossoming roses. Carefully selected from a length of wallpaper, each perfect bloom has been arranged according to its size and colour balance to fit the circular shape.

eye-catching border designs and custom-made friezes can all be created with shapes, or 'motifs' cut from wallpaper. These are ideal for rooms with awkward angles.

The wide range of wallpaper designs available gives you the opportunity to create an individual style, and the chance to highlight (or even disguise!) the shape, or design features of a particular room. An unusual window, like the one pictured, can become a real focal point when surrounded with a design made up from well-chosen

découpage motifs. Plain walls can also be linked to patterned furnishings with a panel motif or border design made up from motifs cut from a co-ordinating wallpaper. This approach offers an original and attractive alternative to the more predictable combination of matching curtains and patterned walls using a single design theme.

Design planning
In planning large-scale découpage designs, first create a strong structural framework of 'key' motifs, then fill in and soften with smaller, secondary elements.

If you have a small amount of wallpaper left over you can use it to decorate accessories. Once you start the fascinating craft of découpage you will find that a single roll of wallpaper can go a long way! The designs can be pasted-on and sealed under layers of varnish in the traditional way, or simply protected with an aerosol sealant.

Choosing wallpaper designs

Changing the position and direction of individual wallpaper motifs offers great scope for découpage design. Many wallpapers have suitable motifs, but there are a few guidelines which you should follow before making a start on any découpage project.

Defined outlines

Printed images with well-drawn outlines are best for cutting out, so choose wallpaper with clearly defined patterns. Small details outside the main design area can be omitted when cutting out the motifs, but any that are included should be easy to handle, and not too frail.

Directional designs

A wallpaper with strongly directional design motifs – where all the motifs appear to face one way – may not work as successfully as a design with a less obvious pattern arrangement, where the motifs flow in different directions.

Floral and leafy patterns are very adaptable, as motifs cut from these can usually be positioned upside down or on their sides and still look good. Figurative designs need more care – a bird motif for instance, will probably have to face the same direction wherever it is used, to avoid looking odd.

Combining papers

Different patterned wallpapers can be combined effectively in a découpage design if the colours and design styles work well together. Many wallpaper ranges include a choice of co-ordinating wallpaper designs with different or smaller scale motifs, and these can be used together in this way.

If using motifs cut from different thicknesses of wallpapers, paste the thinner paper to another to make it the same thickness, as this will improve the appearance of the finished design. Do this by cutting the motif from the thinner wallpaper, allowing a generous area all round the outline, and paste the motif to a backing paper (good quality copy paper is suitable). Press flat under a weight and leave to dry before cutting out the motif neatly.

PREPARING A DESIGN

Materials

Wallpaper Choose medium thickness papers that handle well. Avoid papers with surfaces which mark or crack easily.
Scissors Sharp pointed scissors and curved manicure scissors
Sheets of clean paper, ruler and **pencil**
Coloured pencils or **felt-tip pens** for colouring the cut edges of the paper, to avoid a contrasting light coloured line showing around the edge of the design
Wallpaper paste suitable for chosen wallpaper, **brushes**, **sponge** or **cloth**
Small craft roller to press motifs flat
Acrylic sealer spray for paper (matt finish) to protect surface, and to prevent varnish from penetrating and spoiling the surface. (Available from art shops)
Clear polyurethane varnish (optional) to protect découpaged surfaces – advisable for horizontal designs and accessories
Old newspapers to protect work surfaces

Taking care at the preparation stage pays dividends with the finished design. Follow these tips when cutting the paper shapes so that the overlaps and edges blend well.

1 Strengthening the outline Thinly drawn outlines on a design may need thickening to avoid them disappearing after cutting out. Use a matching coloured pencil to draw round the motif outline, so that it will be easy to follow when you cut it out.

DESIGNING THE MOTIF

The proportions of the découpage design will be influenced by its location, and its balance will be affected by the clever positioning of motifs to create the overall effect.

1 Large and small shapes When working on a three-dimensional object aim to balance the design by placing motifs so that they look good when viewed from different angles.

Start a design with a selection of cut-out motifs in various sizes – more than you think necessary. Try placing shapes at random over the background area. Use a little low-tack putty adhesive to hold them on vertical surfaces and re-arrange them as necessary to reach the desired effect. Place large shapes in position first to balance the composition, and arrange smaller shapes over or under these.

2 Sticking shapes in place Prepare the base surface so it is clean and dry, and mix wallpaper paste following pack instructions. Paste the backs of the motifs, press them in place and wipe away excess paste. When the surface is free of adhesive, remove air bubbles by placing a sheet of clean paper over the design, and smooth the shapes flat with a small roller. Build up the design, re-arranging any shapes while the paste is wet. Leave to dry for at least 24 hours. When you are sure the découpage has dried out apply the acrylic sealer and then one or two coats of clear varnish. The sealer will prevent the varnish from penetrating the paper and spoiling the design.

2 Linking shapes Delicate shapes like fine flower stems can be strengthened to prevent them from tearing when they are eased into position. Make temporary bridges by drawing sections between relevant areas of the design. These can be cut away once the motif is in place.

3 Cutting out Roughly cut round the design leaving a narrow border outside the drawn outline, so shapes are easier to handle. When cutting away interior spaces, use the blade tips of small scissors to pierce a hole, then insert the blades from below and cut round the outline.

4 Bevelling the cut edges Now cut along the outside edge of the design, holding the scissors at a slight angle so that the cut edge slopes to the wrong side of the paper. Thinning the edge in this way helps blend the paper with the background. Colour round the cut edge as before to further disguise the white cut edge.

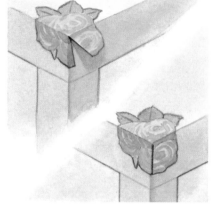

4 External corners When using découpage on box shapes or furniture, it may be necessary to cover a corner – on a table-top, for example – to continue the design 'flow'. The motif can be cut and shaped to fit the corner exactly. Paste the back of the motif, then place it flat to overhang the corner. Snip up to the corner point and fold the cut edges to overlap. Trim the underlap slightly and press the overlap on top of this. The cut edge should be level with the vertical edge. Trim if necessary.

3 Working round angles If the découpage is to be arranged at right angles round an object – a door or window frame, for example – look again at the arrangement of the motifs. Consider whether the design elements can be overlapped attractively round the shape, or whether the angle requires a special treatment – perhaps by placing a larger motif at each corner to accentuate the shape, and create a decorative frame effect.

▶ Floral choice
When you have chosen the wallpapers, cut out a much larger selection of motifs than you think you will need to complete the design. This allows for lots of design options.

Decorative jam pots

Personalise home-made preserves, with these original tops and labels designed to match each other and complement your kitchen. Even shop-bought jams take on a new flavour if displayed in a similar way. If you're lost for a simple gift idea or need to contribute to a worthy bazaar get busy with your scissors and wallpaper scraps.

Materials

Glass jam jars filled with preserve
Cotton gingham fabric scraps
Ribbon selection of lengths and colours to match fabric
Plates and saucers different sizes for templates
Elastic bands
Pencil
Clear adhesive such as Uhu glue.
Découpage motifs or **magazines**
Pinking shears
Sharp pointed paper scissors
Jam pot labels and **pen**

MAKING THE LABELS AND JAM POT COVERS

▲ All home-made
All you need to smarten-up your jam jars are scraps of colourful fabrics, matching ribbon, white card and stylish accessories. These traditional stick-on labels have been prettied up with découpage motifs in colours which complement the gingham covers and ribbons.

1 Cutting out the jam pot cover Iron the fabric and lay it out flat. Using a plate of the correct size as a template for the cover, place it face down on the fabric. With a pencil, draw around the plate, then cut out the circle using pinking shears. If you can't find a suitable plate, use the gingham pattern to cut a square.

2 Cover the jam pot Lay the circle of fabric centrally over the jam jar and pop an elastic band over the cover to keep it in place. Cover the elastic band with a length of ribbon in a colour which matches the fabric, and tie the ribbon to form a bow. Trim the ribbon ends at angles.

3 Preparing the motifs Select a suitable motif and cut it out neatly using the sharp pointed scissors.

4 Labelling the jars Write the contents of the jar on to the label, then, positioning it carefully, stick it on to the jar, then use the clear glue to stick the motif on the jar next to the label, taking care to stick the edges down completely.

◄ Tie a yellow ribbon
For a smaller jar, or for preserves to be given as a present, make a decorated label to fasten to the jar by looping a length of co-ordinated ribbon through a hole in the label, and tying it to the top of the jar.

Découpage gifts

Découpage is an excellent technique for transforming everyday items found in the home into unusual and special treasures. Instead of throwing away empty boxes, tubs and other household cartons, try covering them with charming découpage motifs, to create decorative containers. We used special Victorian scraps, but any good quality paper shapes can be used.

Reusable tissue box
Covering an ordinary tissue box with floral motifs gives an elegant look to a commonplace object. The dainty bow at the front cleverly doubles as a fastening so that the box can be refilled once empty with more tissues. You could make one for the bedroom, and another to tone in with the decor of the guest room or even the bathroom.

▲ A touch of découpage
Transform everyday objects with delicate découpage. Here a co-ordinating tissue box and jewellery tidy have been produced using similar bought scraps, while a tattered photo frame gets a new lease of life decorated with Victorian faces.

Materials
Cube tissue box
Wallpaper paste
Jam jar
Paintbrush 2.5cm (1in)
Découpage motifs or gift paper
Satin finish varnish
Paintbrush 2.5cm (1in) wide
Craft knife
Double sided satin ribbon 1cm (⅜in) x 50cm (19¾in)
Sharp pointed paper scissors
Ruler and **pencil**

MAKING THE TISSUE BOX

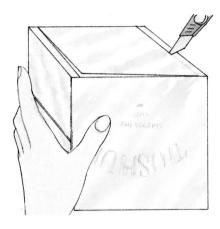

1 Cutting the opening Turn the box upside down and draw two lines 1cm (⅜in) away from and parallel to each side edge. Use the craft knife to cut along the two pencil lines, then cut along one long edge to create a flap. Remove any tissues and keep to one side.

2 Preparing the motifs Select motifs with a similar theme from gift paper or use Victorian-style scraps. Cut out the motifs, working carefully around the intricate shapes so as not to distort them.

3 Sticking the motifs in place Mix the wallpaper paste in the jam jar following the maker's instructions for lining paper, and leave to stand for 5 minutes. Liberally pasting the motifs one at a time, begin by sticking smaller shapes around the top opening of the box. Continue to stick the motifs in place, glueing large motifs over the folds and smoothing them around the corners and under the bottom of the box, for a neat finish. Place small motifs over tiny, awkward or hard to fill spaces, until the surface is completely covered then stick any motifs you wish to display on top.

Picture frame
This particular frame is decorated with purchased motifs made especially for the découpage technique. If you happen to have plenty of spare family snapshots, you could cut out just the head and shoulders of family members to make a more personalised picture frame, but you will need to use a strong clear glue to attach them. Wide frames look best covered with découpage; use a picture mount to help fill the central area if your photo is too small. Alternatively use your découpaged frame for a mirror.

Materials
Chunky picture frame with smooth uncarved sides
Wallpaper paste
Jam jar
Paintbrush 2.5cm (1in) wide
Découpage motifs, magazines or **family snapshots**
Satin finish varnish
Sharp pointed paper scissors

COVERING THE PICTURE FRAME

1 Preparing the motifs Select motifs with a similar theme from magazine pages or a collection of découpage motifs, then cut them out neatly, taking care to avoid distortion, with the sharp pointed scissors.

4 **Varnishing the box** Make sure that all the cutouts have been securely glued in place, particularly around the edges, then leave the box to dry thoroughly. Once dry apply a protective coat of varnish, brushing in one direction only. Leave to dry overnight, then apply a second coat, brushing in a different direction. Again leave until thoroughly dry before adding a further two layers of varnish, as before.

5 **Attaching the ribbon fastening** Mark a point centrally 1.5cm (⅝in) from the opening flap edge under the box. Cut a slit in the flap at the marked position the width of the ribbon. Mark another point on the front of the box in the centre, 2.5cm (1in) up from the base, and cut a second slit. Thread the ribbon through the slit in the flap, making sure that it is not twisted.

6 **Filling the box** Fill the box with tissues, then thread the end of ribbon now on the inner side of the flap up and out through the slit on the front. Pull the ribbon firmly and tie to form a bow at the front. Trim the ends of the ribbon at angles.

2 **Sticking the motifs in place** Mix the wallpaper paste as for the tissue box. Glue the motifs in place all over the surface until none of the original frame can be seen. Take care to stick only small motifs into the corners of the picture frame and to curve the shapes round to the inside and to the back of the frame, to give a smooth neat finish over the complete surface of the frame.

3 **Varnishing the picture frame** Apply several layers of varnish over the picture frame as for the tissue box.

tip

Perfect finish
The addition of extra layers of varnish gives the découpage articles a beautiful sheen, as well as increased strength and durability. Traditionally you can add at least twenty layers of varnish, sanding after every sixth layer with wire wool, in order to create a completely smooth surface.

Add a tray

This small round tray is the perfect way to keep jewellery together. Use a cheese box lid with a flat base and cover with cutout motifs in the same way, to match the tissue box.

A découpage box

A light plywood box has been transformed into an attractive jewellery box with découpage. The pansies have been cut from a sheet of good-quality gift wrap. When choosing a box to decorate, make sure it has a loose-fitting lid as several layers of varnish brushed over the motifs will make it impossible to replace a well-fitting lid. Otherwise you will have to restrict the decoration on the sides to below the lid when it is in position. When planning the design try to continue the motifs on the top over on to the sides of the lid.

You could add motifs to the inside of the box as well, or simply paint the inner surfaces and add a layer of tissue or cotton wool.

Materials
Small unvarnished wooden box with a loose-fitting lid.
Floral wrapping paper, one sheet should be sufficient for a small box.
Glasspaper, sanding block with medium and fine glasspaper.
Wire wool, 000 grade.
Varnish with clear satin finish.
Paint, household emulsion, in colour to match background of wrapping paper.
Paint brushes, 12mm (^{1}/$_2$in) or finer for applying glue, paint and varnish.
Manicure scissors
Transparent craft glue
Clear wax polish
Wallpaper seam roller

▲ **Dressing table collection** Several layers of varnish have been built up to give an antique look to the box.

34

MAKING A DECOUPAGE BOX

1 Preparing the surface Using a sanding block and medium grade glasspaper, rub down the surface of the box. Wipe off the dust.

2 Seal the surface Paint the box and lid with a coat of emulsion paint and leave to dry for at least six hours. Lightly rub over the surface with fine glasspaper.

3 Preparing the motifs Select the flower motifs and carefully cut round each one using a pair of manicure scissors held at a slight angle. This will bevel the edge and help the paper blend into the background. Cut out enough shapes to provide a generous collection to choose from when designing.

4 Work out the design Draw round the lid on a sheet of paper and lay out the cut shapes, moving them about until the arrangement pleases you. Shapes can be overlapped and some of the plain background can show in between the motifs as part of the design.

5 Sticking the shapes in place Stick the largest shapes in place first. Spread the wrong side evenly with glue and press in place. On overlapping sections, leave the edge unstuck so the next shape can slide underneath. Place a sheet of plain white paper over the shape and gently roll it flat with a wallpaper seam roller. Clean off any excess glue squeezed out.

6 Completing the design Continue adding more shapes in the same way. If possible arrange the design so the shapes reach over the edge of both base and lid.

7 Varnishing the design When all the shapes have been securely stuck in place and the glue has dried, apply a coat of varnish. Use varnish sparingly, brushing in one direction. Leave to dry overnight. When dry, add a second coat, brushing in a different direction, and leave to dry overnight.

8 Adding extra layers of varnish When dry, lightly rub all over with fine glasspaper and wipe away the dust. Continue varnishing and lightly rubbing until you have coated the box pieces with between ten and 20 layers of varnish, each brushed in a different direction. The box is complete when the edges of the shapes are smooth to the touch under the layers of varnish.

9 Final coat Finally rub over the surface very gently with fine wire wool. Polish the surface with wax polish using a soft cloth.

► **Floral flowerpot** Decorate round the side of a vase or flowerpot with cut out flower shapes. Keep the design just above the base so that any excess water will not damage the decoration.

▼ **Revive an old tray** Small floral motifs have been used round the edge of this tray with large scale flowers and leaves used to build up a pair of bouquets. The bunches of flowers face in opposite directions so that the tray can be viewed from both sides.

Stamp duty

A rich collection of colourful stamps is the perfect covering for picture frames and small boxes. The stamps are quick to apply and once in position provide a lasting memento of countries visited or friends living abroad. You can use stamps steamed from your everyday mail too, and by jumbling up the different colours you'll still get a picturesque result.

The stamps can be stuck in neat rows across boxes and frames, or overlapped in a riot of colourful confusion on round or unusual shaped objects. Stamps are small enough to mould around the outline of a frame so there is no need for any delicate or intricate trimming. Use the stamps as they are and just layer them to cover any shape.

Stamps can also be used to hide a less-than-perfect article, quickly giving it a brand new look with this fun finish. They need not be confined to boxes and frames, but can be used to convert files and book covers or to alter small chests and cases. Stationery boxes can be easily identified with a layer of stamps and it's the perfect way to frame holiday snaps or photos of pen pals.

▼ *Stamps galore*
Store your treasured letters in a pretty box decorated with stamps collected from home and abroad. Adding torn scraps from favourite letters helps the stamps go further.

COVERING THE FRAME

Materials
Used stamps in a variety of different colours and shapes
Wallpaper paste and **jam jar** for mixing
Small boxes and **picture frames** to cover
Varnish in either satin or matt finish
Paint brushes for paste and varnish

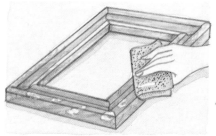

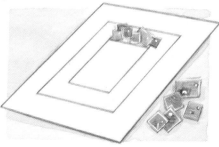

1 Sorting the stamps Soak off stamps from envelopes or postcards by leaving them in a bowl of cold water; once the stamp is free, leave to dry upside down on blotting paper. Divide them into light and dark colours or into special groups.

2 Preparing the frame If an old or second-hand frame is used, lightly sand down the frame surface to remove any odd flakes of paint or varnish. Wipe over the frame with a damp cloth to remove any dust. Lay on newpapers ready for decoration.

3 Working out the design The stamps can be stuck randomly over the frame but if you want a precise design, draw round the frame on a sheet of paper and arrange the stamps inside the marked outline. Use this as a guide.

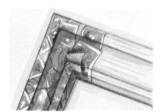

4 Sticking the stamps Mix up a small amount of paste, then using a small brush, evenly paste the wrong side of the first stamp and press on to the frame, making sure it follows the contours of the moulding. Gently smooth over with a cloth to remove air bubbles and excess paste.

5 Covering the frame Continue pasting and sticking the stamps over the frame. Overlap each stamp with the previous one to hide the frame base completely.

6 Neatening the edges It is important to cover the inner and outer edges of the frame so that it looks smart from any angle. Make sure that the stamps overlap the edges all round and stick them on to the wrong side. When the whole frame is covered, leave it to dry.

▶ **Framed with stamps**
Choose a vibrant collection of stamps to cover a frame like this. The stamps mould round the frame shape, bringing it to life and providing the picture with an unusual surround.

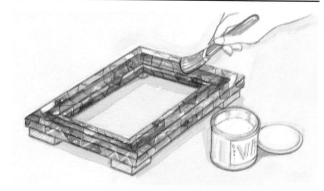

7 Varnish the frame Paint over the whole frame with varnish. When varnishing the frame, place it over four blocks of waste wood so the sides can dry without smudging. Cover with 3 to 4 coats, leaving them to dry between each coat. If necessary, gently rub down with fine glasspaper or wire wool between the last two coats.

COVERING THE BOX

Cover the lid and base of a box separately. If your stamp collection is meagre, cover the box randomly with torn-up letters before adding the stamps. Finally add the protective coats of varnish. To prevent the letter ink from smudging, fix the ink by spraying both sides of the paper with artists' fixative.

tip

Collecting stamps
Small packs of mixed stamps can be purchased quite cheaply from stationery or stamp collector shops. You could try using stamps based around a theme – birds, flowers or castles – or perhaps use stamps in particular colours to complement your home.

Floral firescreen

Whether you have a real coal fire, a gas fire or an electric model, the area around the fireplace can look cold and empty in the summer months when the fire isn't lit. The best way to cheer up this part of the room is to place a traditional, brightly decorated firescreen in front of the fireplace.

The most popular firescreens are traditional floral designs, in which the flowers are 'arranged' in a vase. It is also possible to find bird and animal designs – cats are favourites. Animal firescreens are almost always painted while floral ones can be either painted, or decorated with découpage displays.

Decorative firescreens can be bought ready-made but they are often expensive. Cutting out and decorating a firescreen with a découpage flower display is much cheaper. It is also great fun and very rewarding if you pick floral wallpaper which complements the decor of the room. Spend some time looking at floral pictures in magazines and at reproductions of colour paintings to gather ideas. You can choose from exotic or formal displays to romantic cottage garden styles, either using one favourite wallpaper or a mixture of papers which blend well.

The firescreen itself is made from medium density fibreboard. The pattern is drawn on and cut out using either a coping saw or an electric jigsaw. The découpage flowers are 'arranged' in a vase which is painted on to the board. If you wish, you could decorate the vase with a special paint effect such as marbling or lapis lazuli.

▼ *Hearth warming*
This charming floral firescreen is exactly the right size to cover the fireplace and it stands out well against the brick surround.

A realistic effect is produced by making some of the flowers and leaves overlap the vase edge.

MAKING A DECOUPAGE FIRESCREEN

Materials

Medium density fibreboard (MDF): 1 piece 6mm (¼in) thick, to make the screen and another piece 15mm (⅝in) thick to make the hinged support

Floral wallpaper for the découpage. We used a paper featuring roses and peonies.

PVA glue to stick the flowers to the board

Oil-based primer for the vase, back and edges of the screen

Satin-finish paint suitable for wood, in two colours. This is to paint the white marble effect flower container and the back and side edges of the screen in a toning colour

Polyurethane varnish in a satin finish

Tools: An electric jigsaw or a **coping saw** with a fine blade for cutting round the flower shapes.

Two 4cm (1½in) **butterfly cabinet hinges** for the support

Wood adhesive and **sandpaper**

Paint brushes and **white spirit**

Tracing paper, graph paper, ruler and **pencil**

When making the firescreen, it is best to rest the fibreboard on a table or working surface that is slightly larger than the screen. Move the fibreboard over the edge of this surface before using the saw, to ensure that you don't cut into the table.

1 Sizing the firescreen Measure your fireplace and work out the size of the firescreen. It should be as tall as, and a little wider than the grate area, but it could extend to the width of the fire surround if preferred.

2 Making a pattern Trace the illustrated design on to graph paper, enlarging the pattern to the required size, appropriate to that of your fireplace. Cut out and take the pattern with you to buy the fibreboard. Trace the pattern on to the fibreboard.

3 Cutting out the flowers Carefully cut out lots of flower motifs from your chosen wallpaper. Choose as many different and interesting shapes as possible. If you are using more than one paper, try to choose designs and colours that blend together well.

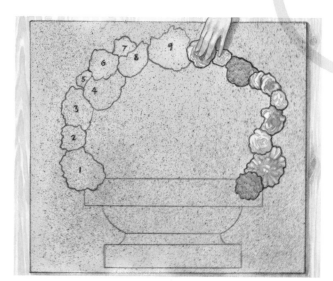

4 Arranging the flower edging Lay out some of the flower cut-outs all around the fibreboard pattern. Carefully draw round the flowers one at a time. After drawing round each one, lift it and number it on the wrong side before laying it aside and giving its drawn outline the same number.

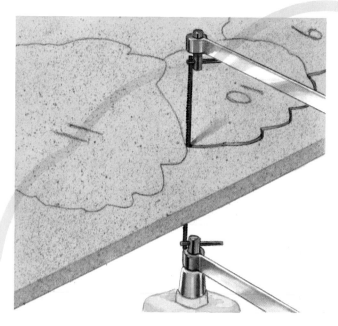

5 Cutting out the firescreen Using an electric jigsaw or a coping saw with a fine blade attached, cut the firescreen out of the fibreboard. Be as careful and precise as possible when cutting around the edges of the flower outlines. Sand smooth as necessary.

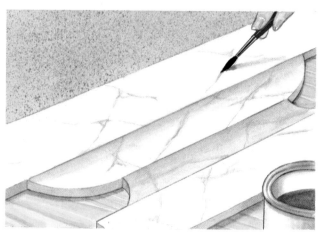

6 Painting the screen Paint in the vase with one undercoat of primer and allow to dry. Then apply a topcoat of satin-finish paint in your chosen colour. Now paint the marble veining effect on to the vase, choosing colours that will complement your room. Feather the edges of the veins to soften the veins for a realistic effect.

Use another colour to paint the back of the firescreen and the cut fibreboard edges, priming the surface first as before. Use a small brush when painting around the edges, to avoid drips. Allow to dry.

tip

Creating marble effects

Instead of painting the vase, you can create the illusion of marble by using sticky-back plastic with a marble finish (available from home decorating stores). This looks exactly like the real thing. Measure and cut the sticky-back plastic into three pieces to fit the three sections of the vase. Stick the pieces on separately to create a realistic marble vase which looks as though it has been chiselled out of three blocks of marble.

7 **Making the découpage** Replace the flower cut-outs around the edge in the same order as before, matching their shape to the cut edge. Stick them in position. Now build up a flower display in the middle. Lay out one group of flowers at a time, trying out layouts before you stick the cut-outs in place. Try to create a realistic effect by positioning some flowers and leaves so that they overlap the edge of the vase.

8 **Protecting the firescreen** Apply one or two coats of varnish over the découpage side of the firescreen. Allow to dry, then varnish the screen back.

▲ Roses and peonies
For the most realistic and effective découpage, choose a wallpaper with a well-drawn, detailed flower design. Then create an interesting collage effect by placing smaller shapes over larger ones, and putting together contrasting colours and shapes.

Leaves can be used to 'break up' flower groups and they also lend themselves well to positioning so that they overlap the vase.

▶ On a roll
You may have some suitable wallpaper remnants at home, but if not there are plenty of beautiful designs to choose from in the shops.

Sticky-back plastic for the marble effect can be bought by the metre (yard) from home decorating stores.

MAKING A HINGE FOR THE FIRESCREEN

1 **Making a hinge** Lie the firescreen flower side down and measure and mark a line down the centre of the back. Cut two pieces of MDF 15mm (⅝in) thick, as shown, adapting the size to fit the firescreen.

2 **Attaching the support** Using adhesive, stick the support piece (**A**) on to the back of the firescreen in line with the centre mark. Weight the support with a heavy book or bricks until the adhesive has set firmly.

Pattern for firescreen support

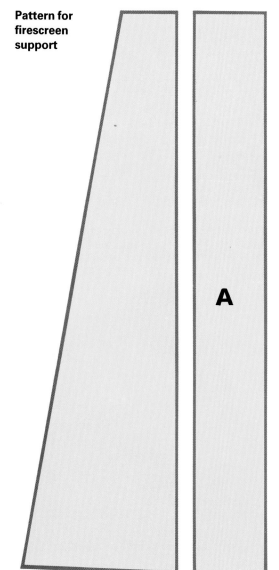

A

3 **Fixing the hinge** Sand off any excess glue around the support. With the screen flat against a wall, hold up the remaining piece of board to the support and mark hinge positions on both pieces. Screw the hinge components into place.

Finally stand the firescreen up and varnish the cut edges using a small brush. Leave to dry.

tip

Support template
Enlarge the support template pieces shown here to fit the back of your screen.

Photocopy printing

By photocopying images on to plain, patterned or coloured paper, you can create your own découpage designs which, when applied to walls and objects around the home, will produce an inexpensive, yet effective, transformation. Although the idea is surprisingly simple, the results can be stunning. Try something easy at first, and once you have mastered the basics, you can start experimenting by adding colours or using textured paper.

Specialist book shops stock hundreds of books of decorative motifs from old woodcuts and engravings to illustrations which are all now out of copyright, so the designs are easy to obtain. Whether you lean towards Art Nouveau borders, floral motifs, old Delft tile designs or William Morris patterns, there are styles to suit every taste.

You can either use the images to cover an area, or as a random decoration. So you can literally create your own wallpaper or personalise belongings and update furniture; the possibilities are endless and the choice is up to you.

▼ Mix and match motifs
These botanical prints have been photocopied on to A3 sheets of lining paper and applied to the walls. Photocopies of old accountancy records have been used to cover the table, while vegetable designs have been used to decorate smaller items.

DECORATING A WALL

Materials
Motifs of your choice
Sheets of coloured paper to match, or contrast with your walls
Craft knife
Wallpaper paste and **small brush**
Glaze made with five parts PVA to one part water
Small sponge
Washing-up bowl
Paint brush

This attractive leaf design was photocopied on to yellow paper to match the colour of the paint on the walls. The design was photocopied in a variety of sizes, then cut out and pasted on. It is easier to use a craft knife and cutting board to cut out any fiddly designs, rather than trying to use scissors.

1 Preparing the designs Photocopy your chosen design on to coloured paper to match or contrast with your walls. If you can only find white paper, paint or colour in your designs to co-ordinate with your colour scheme. Cut round each one carefully, using a sharp craft knife.

2 Fixing the designs Mix up some wallpaper paste and carefully brush a small amount over the back of each design, one at a time. Arrange the motifs in a random pattern over the wall.

3 Smoothing out faults Wet the sponge until it is just moist. Then gently stroke over each design, working from the middle outwards, to smooth out any bubbles and remove any excess wallpaper paste. Take care to use a light touch, so that the designs are not disturbed.

4 Sealing the wall Allow the designs to dry out completely. Then, using the washing-up bowl, mix up the glaze, consisting of five parts matt emulsion PVA glaze to one part water. Apply an even coat over all the wall. Allow to dry.

DECORATING THE FLOOR

Materials
Photocopied designs cut out with a craft knife
Wallpaper paste and **brush**
Clear, matt polyurethane varnish
Paint brush
Sponge
Washing-up bowl

These leaf motifs create a stunning display, strewn across the skirting board and on to the floor like fallen leaves in autumn. As these areas are liable to take a lot of wear, several layers of varnish are needed to protect the designs and keep them in good condition.

1 Laying the designs Carefully brush a little wallpaper paste over the reverse side of your designs, as before. Position motifs and smooth out any faults with the sponge. Allow to dry.

DECORATING FABRIC

Materials
Transfer paint
Tin foil
Paint brush
Sponge
Paper towel

Using transfer paint, photocopied designs can be applied to fabrics, as this stunning silk throw illustrates. The paint reverses the image, so select pictures without words or numbers. The chemicals give the fabric a plastic feel, so experiment first.

1 Preparing the fabric Place a piece of foil under the design area to prevent any of the transfer paint from seeping through.

2 Applying the image Following manufacturer's instructions, brush a generous amount of the transfer paint on to the right side of your design. Place this on to your fabric, pasted side down. Blot away excess paste.

2 Fixing the designs Varnish over the entire area, taking extra care when covering the designs. Allow to dry thoroughly, then repeat the process, applying at least six coats.

▶ Falling leaves
A pretty leaf motif has been photocopied in various sizes on to yellow paper, cut out and pasted over a wall painted the same colour. The design also falls across the skirting board and on to the floor, providing a stunning contrast to the white floorboards.

3 Revealing the image Place a wet sponge on to the image and allow the water to soak through for a few minutes until the paper is thoroughly wet. Begin rubbing gently in the centre of the paper until it can be rolled off to reveal the transferred image.

4 Sealing the image Apply a few drops of the transfer paint on to your image and rub gently into the grain with a paint brush. Make sure that the entire surface of the design is moistened. Allow to dry out thoroughly.

Design ideas

Once you have seen how simple photo-copy printing is, there will be lots of projects you will want to undertake using this technique. There is a wide variety of papers you can use, and unwanted areas of your design can just be erased with correction fluid.

Try using photocopied motifs in a collage, or use them for découpage effects – from furniture to frames, the possibilities are endless.

◀ Personalised invitations
The photocopy printing technique can be used just as effectively to decorate notepaper, party invitations or even change of address cards. You can photocopy the image you want directly on to the paper, or cut out the image and glue it into place.

The picture frame shown here started life as a plain piece of cardboard. It was covered with several layers of papier mâché and, finally, with torn pieces of photocopied prints. The sepia colour was achieved by sponging down the frame with tea.

▶ Papier mâché decorations
Both made from papier mâché, this desk tidy and small bowl have been decorated with photocopied designs and then sealed with a clear gloss polyurethane varnish. Once the papier mâché has set, you can glue on appropriate designs: bunches of flowers for a pot pourri container; letters of the alphabet for a desk tidy, or pictures of jewellery or perfume bottles for a bowl on a dressing table. (For details on papier mâché, see pages 23–24.)

◀ Decorating shelves *Small motifs can be functional as well as decorative. Here, photocopies of strawberry fruits have been carefully cut out and glued on to a paper shelf trim as a simple decoration; you could also colour the strawberries in if you wished.*

Why not decorate jars of home-made preserves in the same way? Here, soft fruit designs have been coloured using a poster paint wash, cut out and used as labels on jars of the corresponding fruit jam, along with a record of the year of bottling. A coloured photocopy of raspberries has also been transferred on to one of the jam-pot covers as a colourful reminder of what type of fruit jam is inside.

Pleated paper blind

Attractive and quite simple to make, pleated paper can be transformed into a variety of objects. Paper blinds, for example, can be a versatile alternativ to the more conventional fabric variety, and are also surprisingly durable. They are ideal for small windows where only one sheet of paper is needed, but larger blinds can be made by simply adding more sheets of paper.

The paper is folded in a concertina-fashion to the width and depth of the window, with the folds either close together to form narrow pleats, or wider apart for deeper folds. Blinds are attached to the window frame with a strip of Velcro, and are pulled up and down with a simple cord mechanism.

Pleated paper can be made in as many colours and patterns as there are sheets of wrapping paper. Even fine, handmade papers can be used, mounted on to thicker sheets so that they retain their delicate translucent qualities.

▼ Paper mates
Here, a blind and lampshade have been made using co-ordinating pleated paper. The paper for the blind is trimmed to fit the window.

MAKING A PLEATED BLIND

Materials

Wrapping paper See steps for quantities
Cartridge paper See steps for quantities
Spray adhesive
Long metal ruler and pencil
Knitting needle
Hole punch
PVC hole reinforcements
Scissors
Thick card
Blind cord
Stick 'n' stick Velcro
Wood 4.5cm (1¾in) x 2cm (¾in) x width of blind
3 eyelets
Light-pull acorn
Cleat hook
Newspaper
2 L-shaped brackets

The techniques needed to make these blinds are not complicated, but success will depend upon the proper measuring and scoring of the pleats.

1 Measuring up To find the amount of paper required, measure the outside edges of the window. The finished blind will be the width of the window so, depending on the size of your paper and window, you may need to join sheets together.

Calculate the length of paper needed by adding on an extra third to the depth measurement. Adjust this to the nearest figure divisible by 8cm (3¼in), allowing for 4cm (1½in) pleats. Add another 20cm (7¾in) for the top and bottom turnings.

2 Stiffening the wrapping paper Protecting surfaces with newspaper, spray the cartridge paper evenly with adhesive. Carefully lay the wrapping paper over the lining paper, right side up, and smooth together, making sure there are no wrinkles. Trim to fit.

3 Joining sheets of paper If you are using more than one width of paper, stick these sheets together with spray adhesive before you begin. Make sure that any patterns match before you join together.

4 Mark and score the first sheet On the back of the paper, using the long metal ruler and the knitting needle, measure and score the first line 12cm (4¾in) down from the top of the paper, across the width. Continue scoring parallel lines every 4cm (1½in) to the end of the sheet.

▶ **Pleats in reserve**
When calculating the length of the blind, allow for extra folds, so the blind is never completely extended.

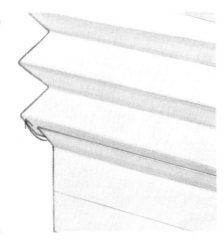

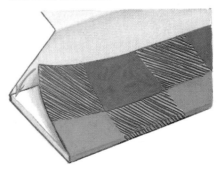

6 Folding the paper Starting at the top, make concertina pleats along your scored lines, leaving the last two lines unfolded.

5 Adding the second sheet To add length to the blind, attach another sheet along the bottom short edge of the paper. Spray the edges to be joined with adhesive, making sure that you match up any patterns before you finally position them together. Continue scoring the parallel lines every 4cm (1½in) from the last score line until this second sheet is also completed. Using the ruler and pencil, measure a sixth of the way in from each long edge and draw a line as a guide for the holes.

7 Finishing the bottom edge Cut a 3.5cm (1½in) strip of card the same width as the paper. Stick across the bottom edge of the blind with spray adhesive, enclosing the card within the last two folds of the blind. Secure with more adhesive.

8 Punching the holes With the wrong side of the blind facing you, punch a hole at the centre of each pleat, in the middle of the drawn line on both sides of the blind. Reinforce each hole with a PVC ring.

9 Attaching the top edge With the wrong side facing, score one line across the blind 2cm (¾in) down from the top and another one 5cm (2in) down from that. Cut a 4.5cm (1¾in) strip of card the same width as the blind. Stick in place and enclose as for the bottom edge.

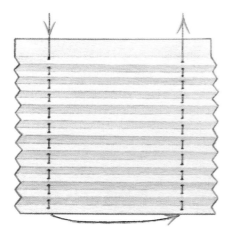

10 Threading the cord Thread the blind cord down through the holes on one side of the blind, across the bottom and up through the holes on the other side. Leave ends loose.

11 Making the fastening strip Cut a wooden strip the width of the blind. Screw the eyelets into the long narrow edge, to match up with the holes in the blind. As a guide for the cord, attach the third eyelet to the wooden strip at either the right or left edge of the blind, depending on which side the cord is to hang.

12 Attaching the Velcro Stick the hook side of the Velcro strip to the top edge of the wooden strip, furthest away from the eyelets on the long flat side. Stick the fuzzy side along the top back edge of the blind.

13 Attaching to the window frame Screw the wooden strip to the top of the window frame using the L-brackets. Attach the blind with the Velcro. Thread the cord through both the eyelets in the wooden strip. One piece of cord will travel through both eyelets, depending on which side the cord is to hang.

14 Finishing the cording Thread both ends of the cord through the third eyelet and pull the cord so that the ends are an equal length. Thread through the light-pull acorn and secure with a knot.

15 Attaching the cleat hook Screw the cleat hook to the window frame halfway down on the side the cord is to hang. Wind the cord around this to secure the blind.

tip

Joining paper
Joins between sheets should be as unobtrusive as possible. When working with translucent papers, it is advisable to butt-join them on top of a backing paper. Heavier papers can be joined with an overlap at the back of a pleat.

Choosing papers

There is an almost endless variety of papers to choose from. Oriental designs, with their subtle colours and textures, are enhanced when set against the light and so are ideal for paper blinds. These and other unusual and handmade papers, such as Italian marble designs, are available from specialist shops.

There is no reason to stick to one kind of paper either. Mount torn strips of finer paper on to a cartridge paper backing before pleating, for an interesting effect.

In a myriad of colours, cellophane can also be used if carefully mounted over a thicker paper. Experiment by pleating papers first to avoid any that will crack when creased into pleats.

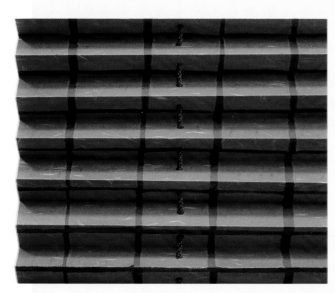

PLEATED LAMPSHADE

Materials

Wrapping paper 1 sheet
A1 cartridge paper 1 sheet
Spray adhesive
Scissors
Metal ruler and pencil
Double-sided tape
Knitting needle
Hole punch
PVC hole reinforcements
Cord
3mm (⅛in) ribbon 70cm (⅞yd)
5mm (¼in) ribbon 40cm (½yd)
Wide-eyed needle
7.5cm (3in) bulb clip
Scalpel or craft knife

Why not team your blind with a matching lampshade? In very little time you can give your room a smart, co-ordinated look. Add a coloured ribbon or delicate lace trim for a finishing touch.

1 Lining and cutting the paper Line the wrapping paper as in *Making a pleated blind, Step 1* on page 48. Make sure that any printed words on the right side of the paper are removed. Measure and mark with a pencil two 16cm (6¼in) wide strips on the wrong side across the length of the paper. Cut out.

2 Sticking and scoring the paper Join the two pieces together by overlapping the short sides by 2cm (¾in) and sticking them together with double-sided tape. With the wrong side facing, use the knitting needle and ruler to measure and score lines across the width of the paper every 2cm (¾in).

3 Folding the paper Make sure that the paper join will be on an inside fold by counting score lines from the join to the start of the strip, and calculating whether the first strip is an outer or an inner fold. Pleat the whole length of the strip up in a concertina fashion.

4 Punching holes Punch holes in the centre of each pleat, 1cm (½in) down from the top edge. Back each hole with a PVC ring.

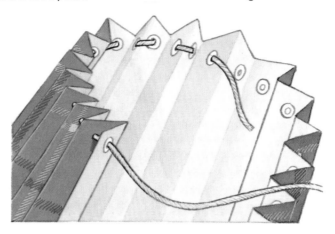

5 Making the shade Join the two edges so they overlap along one fold to make a cylinder. Stick this down with double-sided tape. Then, thread thin cord through the holes and gather the folds by pulling the cord tightly until the top of the shade is the same size as the top of the bulb clip. Carefully and firmly stitch the ends of the cord together to keep the top of the shade permanently that size.

6 Attaching the bulb clip Stick the narrower ribbon to the top ring of the bulb clip and thread on to a wide-eyed needle. Wind the ribbon once around the bulb clip and then once around a piece of cord visible between the folds, again around the clip and then around the next visible piece of cord, and so on around the shade, thereby attaching the bulb clip to the shade.

7 Hiding the cord Thread the larger piece of ribbon through the holes in the same way as the cord, so that it hides the cord from sight. Secure neatly.

▲ *Perfect pleats* The tartan shade sits elegantly on top of a cream stand, which has been delicately crackle-glazed, to add subtlety.

Marbling paper

Decorated with an exquisite mix of colours and individual patterns, marbled papers can be used to cover a wide variety of objects from notebooks and desk sets to boxes and lampshades.

Paper marbling is an ancient technique which originated in the far East and then spread into Europe along the silk routes. The designs are created by floating coloured paints on thickened water then transferring them to paper. The patterns obtained, which include veining, spattering, feathering and swirling are derived from the natural patterns of marble itself.

Although best suited to paper, the technique can work with other objects such as candles, eggs and silk scarves.

▲ Cool co-ordination
The swirling patterns of the marbled paper look equally good pleated into a lampshade or set against the naturally-occuring pattern in a wooden frame. No two pieces of marbled paper can ever be exactly the same, although similar sheets can be made if the same colours and technique are used to decorate them.

Different marbling methods

There are two different types of marbling. One uses water-based colours, to create a very sharp image; the other uses oil-based colours for a softer finish. This is the simplest method of marbling, and works on the basis that water and oil do not mix.

It is possible to create patterns by simply using oil paints on water alone, but for more detailed patterns it is better to thicken the water with glue. The best glue to use is brown school glue which is available from most stationery stores. The glue adds body to the water so that it holds the paint more steadily on its surface. This makes it easier to capture and hold a pattern on the paper.

Spatter patterning is straightforward and a good technique to start with. After a little practice you can try more adventurous designs which require some skill. These include swirling the paint into an imaginative design with a brush and using a marbling comb for feathering.

Materials

Paper Cartridge or tinted papers are best, but any medium-thickness paper will do

Container You can use any watertight container for the paper. Try a roasting tin, developing tray or cat litter tray

Brown, school glue to create the size. It is best to add the glue to the water to a ratio of 1:6. Wallpaper paste can be used as an alternative (½oz to 2pts)

Paints Small tubes of artist's oil paints are ideal. These can be bought in most art shops

White spirit for thinning the paints

Brushes Small paint brushes are needed for spattering the paint

Small tins or **jars for mixing paints**

Tools A thin stick, knitting needle and wide-toothed comb or marbling comb

Waste paper

Making a marbling comb

It is possible to create a regular, well-defined pattern by dragging a metal comb steadily across the surface of the water. Making your own comb is easy. All you need is cardboard, pins, low tack putty and glue. Cut two pieces of cardboard 23cm (9in) x 3.5cm (1in). Put a strip of low adhesive putty along one edge and press steel dressmaker's pins into it, with the sharp ends pointing outwards. Apply adhesive along the card above the line of putty and press the second piece of cardboard over the top. For alternative effects you could make several combs with the teeth spaced differently.

pots for mixing

wallpaper size

brushes

oil paints

cartridge paper

marbling comb

MARBLING PAPER

1 Preparing the tank Half fill your chosen container with 2 litres (3 pints) of water and add 300ml (½ pint) of brown glue, mixing well to create the size.

2 Mixing the paints Squeeze about 2.5cm (1in) of oil paint into a cup and mix with white spirit so the mixture is very thin. You should mix all the colours you think you will need at this stage and set them aside in small pots or jars for later use.

3 Adding the paint Using the paintbrush, spatter small specks of the diluted paint evenly across the surface of the sized water, laying down the base colour first. Add further colours as desired; two or three are normally sufficient.

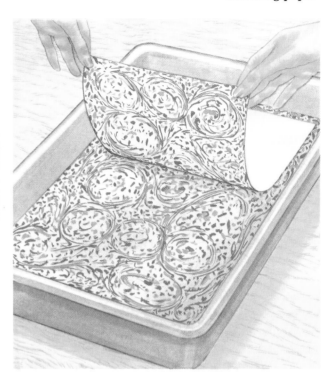

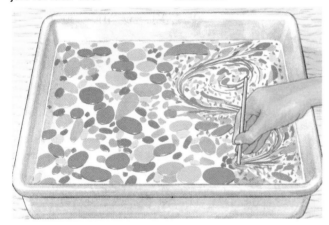

4 Creating the pattern Using the stick or knitting needle, blend and manipulate the colours into a pattern. Alternatively, draw the comb across the surface to create a variety of distinctive designs.

5 Marbling the paper Once satisfied with your pattern, carefully lower a sheet of paper on to the surface. The paper should not be dropped suddenly; the action should be smooth to avoid the appearance of air bubbles. Hold the paper at each end and allow the curved centre of the sheet to touch the water first.

6 Removing the paper Gently peel the paper away from the surface immediately, scraping it across the edge of the tray to remove excess size. Lay face up on a sheet of waste paper to dry.

7 Repeating the process Some paint will remain on the surface and it is often possible to make a second and even a third paler print from this. Just blend the colours together a little to form another pattern. Alternatively, clean the residue away by drawing strips of waste paper across the surface before starting again with newly spattered paint.

8 Drying the paper After about an hour and a half, the marbled paper will be dry enough to move. However you should be careful how you handle it because it will take at least a day to dry completely. Cover the finished piece of work with clean paper and flatten it by pressing it carefully underneath, or in-between the pages of some heavy books.

Pencil power

A pencil pot and pencils covered in marbled paper will make an attractive accessory or ideal gift. The pencils can all be covered in the same colour paper or a variety to create a bright display.

Measure the height and circumference of your container, and cut a piece of marbled paper to fit, allowing a 1cm (⅜in) overlap at the top and sides. Spray the paper with adhesive and wrap around the pot aligning the lower edge of the paper with the base and snipping the top overlap level with the pot. Press the overlap down inside.

Use a rectangle of co-ordinating plain coloured or leatherette paper, 6mm (¼in) shorter than the height for the lining. Spray and attach to the inside. Cut a circle of paper to fit the bottom of the pot. Spray and fit.

For the pencils, cut out marbled paper to cover, spray and stick.

▲ It's a gift!
Giftbags and boxes are a great alternative to giftwrap. Made from paper that you have decorated yourself, they will add a personal touch to any present. They are ideal for wrapping several gifts at once, tackling an awkward object or disguising an obvious shape.

▼ Pastel paper
Say it with more than words! Design your own marbled writing paper and envelopes. The process can be repeated a few times if you want to produce a very pale pattern. This paper has been prettily bordered with a delicate marbled pattern in one colour. Together with the envelopes, the set makes a special gift.

Glamorous gift wraps

If you have more dash than cash this Christmas try wrapping up your gifts in these stunning covers. They look as if they cost a million dollars but they can be made on a budget using discarded shoe boxes, plain packing paper and scraps from your sewing box and garden. It's the idea that counts.

Each of these gift wraps is easy to make but the secret to success is to work neatly and with strong images. The carrier bag with the cut out star is a particularly good example and looks really smashing if there is a cheeky,

cuddly bear peeping out through the window. The pop-up Christmas tree ideas would work equally well using a snowman or shooting star motif.

Enlarge or reduce the size of the motifs, on the graph pattern overleaf, to a size that suits your gift. The pattern can then be traced on to the wrap and cut out or alternatively you can make up a cardboard template. This is especially helpful if you need to draw up the motif several times on each gift wrap.

Let your imagination run wild and mix and match these ideas to create

▲ **Sparkling Christmas wrap**
Wrapped in dazzling Christmas colours of green and silver these presents look a million dollars, but will only take a little time and a few pence to produce. Transform plain carrier bags and boxes into expensive looking gifts everyone will want to unwrap.

more stunning wraps for the presents around your tree. Remember the best wrapped presents are tailor made to suit the personality of the persons who will receive them.

THE CARRIER BAG

Materials
Metallic gift carrier bag
Silver glitter paint
Double-sided adhesive tape
Clear acetate film or white paper to back cut-out star
Craft knife
Cutting board or spare card

The cut-out star in this carrier bag can be either backed with clear acetate to make a window, so that you can peep in or lined with paper in contrasting colour.

1 Cutting out star Place the cutting board inside the bag, then using the large star template and craft knife cut out a star from the centre front. Decorate the cut edge with glitter paint or glue and glitter dust.

2 Backing the star Cut a 15cm (6in) square of white paper or clear acetate film. Stick a piece of double-sided tape to each corner and stick the sheet inside the bag centrally behind the star.

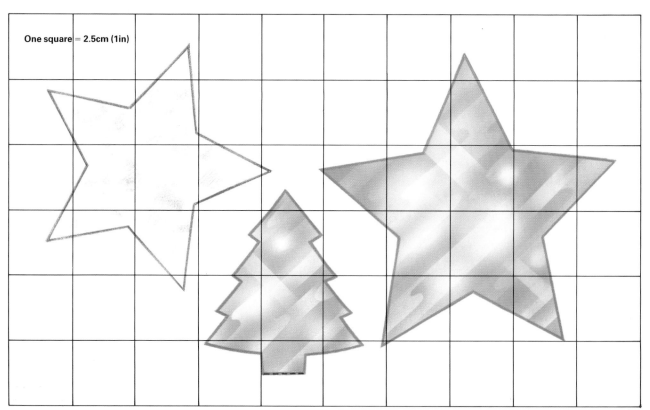

One square = 2.5cm (1in)

THE TREE BOX

Materials
Green metallic paper to wrap box
Thin card or **white paper** to wrap around the parcel
Double-sided adhesive tape
Pinking shears
Craft knife

These pop-up Christmas trees, and similar motifs, make an impressive topping for a box-wrapped gift.

1 Wrapping green box Wrap box with green metallic paper and fasten edges neatly in place.

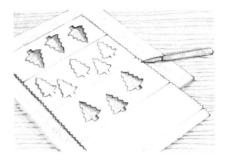

3 Cutting out trees Use the tree template to draw trees on front, back and top areas of paper. Cut out trees on top along solid lines and score along dashed base line. Cut out trees on front and back.

4 Attaching white paper Wrap white paper around box, matching foldlines with edges of the box. Overlap ends on base of box and stick in place with double-sided tape. Stand up trees on top of box.

2 Preparing white paper Cut white paper to wrap around box with a 2.5cm (1in) overlap. Using pinking shears, trim side edges 1cm (⅜in) narrower than box at each side. Wrap paper around box with overlap at base and mark the folds at each corner lightly in pencil. Score along foldlines, so paper folds sharply.

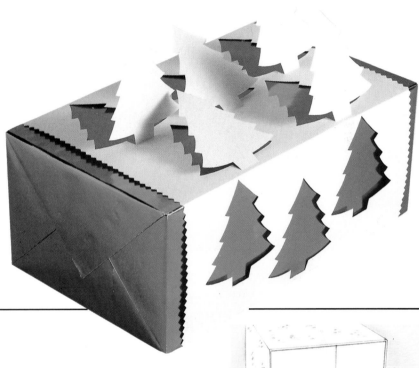

THE SPONGED STAR BOX

Materials
Box suitably sized for the gift
Silver craft paint
Small natural sponge
Silver gift-wrapping ribbon 20cm (8in) of narrow width
Shredded silver foil to fill behind cut-out star
Adhesive tape
Scrap paper
Craft knife
Hole punch

Shoe boxes can be used as the basis for this giftwrap, but it is a good idea to paint them white before you start to decorate them.

1 Sponging the box Spread silver paint on the piece of scrap paper. Take a dab of paint on to the sponge and dab onto the box at random. Repeat, until box is evenly dappled. Leave to dry.

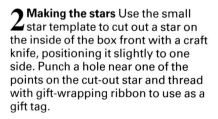

2 Making the stars Use the small star template to cut out a star on the inside of the box front with a craft knife, positioning it slightly to one side. Punch a hole near one of the points on the cut-out star and thread with gift-wrapping ribbon to use as a gift tag.

3 Attaching gift tag Fasten the ends of ribbon inside top edge of box with adhesive tape so the gift tag hangs outside, alongside the cut-out star. Place shredded foil in box behind cut-out star, before adding the gift.

THE BOTTLE WRAP

Materials
Corrugated paper height of bottle plus 3cm (1¼in) and long enough to wrap round bottle
Gold cord 60cm (¾yd) long
Gold braid 70cm (⅞yd) long
Gold tassles two
Sewing thread to match braid
Clear adhesive

Favourite drinks make good presents but can be difficult to pack. Corrugated paper not only looks smart it protects the contents too and the gift wrap can so easily be decorated with bits and pieces from your sewing box.

1 Preparing the paper
Peel the flat backing off the corrugated paper. With the paper flutes running vertically trim the top two corners to curves.

2 Gluing the paper Wrap paper around bottle and glue edges together from base to neck. Glue cord round top and curved edges of paper tucking inner end of cord down between the neck and outer edge.

3 Tying braid Squeeze the paper around the neck of bottle. Wrap braid around bottle neck from front and tie in a knot at back. Bring ends of braid back round to front and knot loosely. Stitch tassles to ends of braid.

▲ **Plain and simple** Even plain brown paper can be turned into stunning giftwraps with a touch of Christmas glitter in the form of gold braids and tassles and winter foliage gathered from the garden.

THE BROWN PARCEL

Materials
Brown parcel paper
Florists foam
Silk berries, leaves, seed pods and **cinnamon sticks**
Wired ribbon
Clear adhesive and **wire**
Double-sided adhesive tape

Fresh foliage can be used to decorate this giftwrap but it will only keep fresh for about a week.

1 Cover the parcel Wrap the parcel in brown paper, turning in the ends neatly. Stick in place with adhesive tape. Turn the parcel so one of the turned-in ends is on top. Stick the florist's foam centrally on top.

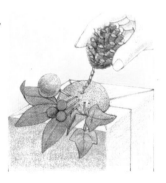

2 Bend ribbon into bows, then wrap wire round the centre of bows, sticks and cones to form a support. Now fix the foliage, seed pods and ribbon bows into the foam. Push in the large items first and arrange the small pieces all round until the top is covered.

Novel notebooks

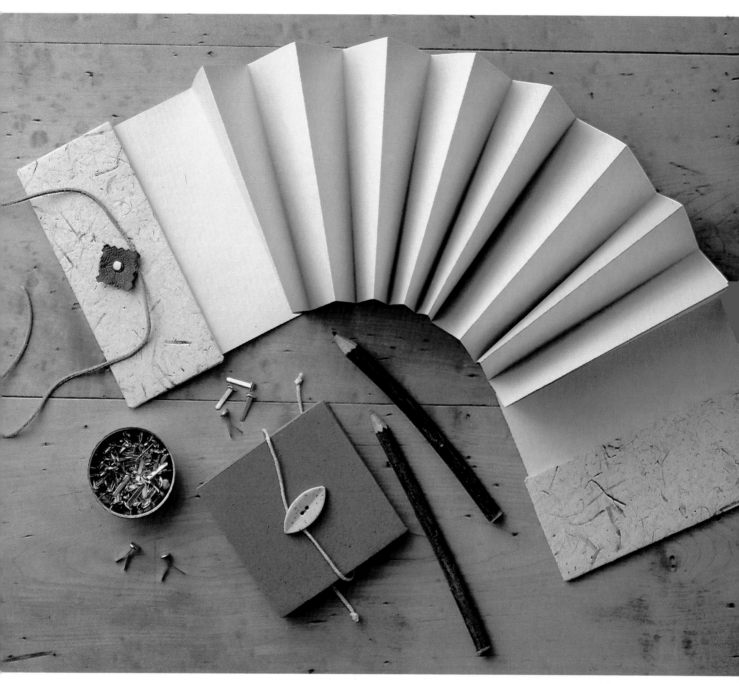

▲ Concertina notepads
Unfold the pages to note down important messages, then tie round each pad with thonging.

Keeping track of all your appointments, notes and messages can be a problem in any busy life. There seem to be so many activities that need to be fitted into each day, and often there are times and points to remember for each activity, so it is useful to have somewhere to jot down your own messages as timely reminders.

Help is at hand in the shape of these smart notebooks. One can be placed by the telephone, the other is thin enough to slip into your handbag or pocket. These two pads look smart and professional enough to attend any meeting

and would make inexpensive, but very stylish presents for family and friends.

We picked a recycled paper for the cover of the long notepad and a plain brown wrapping paper for the cover of the square pad. For the inside pages use a length of wallpaper lining paper, which gives you the opportunity to add as many leaves inside each pad as you feel is appropriate.

Materials
Mounting board
Textured or recycled paper
Wallpaper lining paper
Spray adhesive
All-purpose household glue
Brass paper fastener, scrap of leather
and card
Pinking shears
Leather thonging 50cm (½yd)
Craft knife
Pencil and ruler
Chenille needle
Hammer
Scissors

LONG NOTEPAD

1 Cutting out the covers For the outside covers of the notepad, cut out two pieces of mounting board so that each one measures 17 x 7cm (6¾in x 2¾in). Also cut out two pieces of textured paper so that each one measures 20 x 10cm (8 x 4in). This is for covering the card pieces.

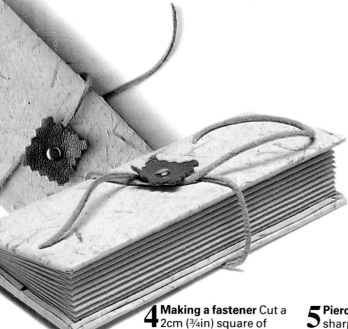

2 Covering the covers Spray adhesive over wrong side of one piece of paper. Place one piece of mounting board centrally on paper. Press in each corner over mounting board, then turn and press over the edges, sticking firmly. Repeat, to make up a second end.

3 Folding pages Cut a strip of lining paper 132 x 16cm (52¼ x 6¼in). Mark long edges into 6cm (2⅜in) sections. Fold the paper along first two marks; crease firmly. Then fold in the opposite direction and crease. Concertina the remainder of the strip in this way.

4 Making a fastener Cut a 2cm (¾in) square of card. Cut a 2.5cm (1in) square of leather with pinking shears. Stick card to leather centre.

5 Piercing holes Use a sharp needle and hammer to pierce hole in centre of one card end. Pierce a similar hole in centre of leather square.

6 Fixing the fastener With right side uppermost, insert a paper fastener through leather square then through the card cover. Spread prongs on wrong side and glue.

Telephone notepad

Cut two 10cm (4in) squares of mounting board and cover with two 13cm (5¼in) squares of textured brown paper. Cut a strip of lining paper 198 x 9cm (77 x 3½in) and carefully fold up concertina style into 9cm (3½in) square pages. Fasten the notepad with a button. Place the button centrally on cover front and mark through the holes with a sharp chenille needle. Sew on the button with a double thread; knot the thread ends together at the back and seal with adhesive against the back of the cover. Complete the notepad in the same way as before, binding it with a length of string.

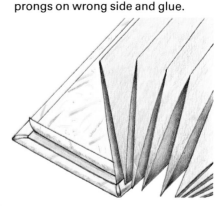

7 Sticking in the pages Stick the first page of the concertina paper centrally over the wrong side of pad front. Then glue the last page centrally over the wrong side of the back cover. Cut two pieces of textured paper 16.5 x 6.5cm (6½ x 2½in). Stick over the concertina sheet to neaten.

8 Binding up the notepad Bind the leather thonging round the notepad and knot round the central leather square to hold.